THAWING FROZEN FROGS

BRIAN PATTEN

Illustrated by
CHRIS RIDDELL

F

FRANCES LINCOLN
CHILDREN'S BOOKS

Contents

The Experiment

I did an experiment to prove that parents
Don't pay much attention.

To my mum I said,
'Gran's just gone and bitten the canary's
    head off!'

She said,
'Well, I never.'

Then to my dad I said,
'The cat's trying to fry a mouse
    for its dinner!'

And he said,
'Well, I never.'

Then I dashed out of the house yelling,
'There's a gigantic elephant just about
    to fall on the roof!'

And they both said,
'Well, I nev-'

SPLAT!!!

The Giant's Family Dinner

For dinner I had a little boy,
He tasted rather funny.
I spat him out right away
Because his nose was runny.

Next I tried a little girl
(They are supposed to taste nicer)
But I broke my tooth because
I'd forgotten to de-ice her.

By now I was quite peckish
So I tried a leg-of-Dad
But it was past the sell-by date
And tasted rather bad.

I nibbled on a mother,
But wanting something new
I boiled a bit of Granny
And tried some Uncle-stew.

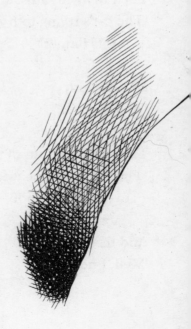

I did not eat the baby –
That was out the question
(And anyway they wriggle
And cause indigestion).

Usually I eat alone
In a huge and draughty hall.
Having a family for dinner
Is not to my taste at all.

The Invisible Man's Invisible Dog

My invisible dog is not much fun.
I don't know if he's glad or glum.
I don't know if, when I pat his head,
I'm really patting his bum instead.

Hairy Fairy

I saw a hairy fairy
Doing press-ups in the gym.
He sweated quite profusely
So I went and said to him,
'Though you are sensational
I find it irrational
To see a hairy fairy
Panting so profusely
With his track-suit hanging loosely
Doing press-ups in the gym.'

The Teachercreature

We held a séance in the kitchen,
Me, Jenny and Jo.
We covered the table with an old stained cloth
And turned the lights down low.
We summoned up a poltergeist,
A witch and a wizard too,
We summoned up a goblin
And an imp or two.
We summoned up a vampire,
A werewolf and a ghoul,
We summoned up a banshee
With a fearful howl.
Our hair turned grey, our knees gave way,
We trembled and felt sweaty.
And then we went and summoned up
A zombie and a yeti.
We summoned up a spectre,
A phantom and a spook,
We summoned up things so bad
We were scared to look.
Then last of all we summoned up
The world's most frightful creature.
We dashed out of the room because
It was our old schoolteacher.

The Owl's Trick
(After Aesop)

From its hollow and ancient tree
An owl looked down and said to me:

'About my feet are swarms of mice –
I can easily leave them there,
For from their feet I've ripped their toes
And now they'll not go anywhere.

I eat them slowly at my ease,
I pick and choose them as I please.
The fattest one I let digest
Before indulging in the rest.

I bring them corn into my croft,
It keeps them both alive and soft.
Before this trick occurred to me
They were nimble and scurried free.

I've neatly torn the paws from each
Panicking creature in my reach;
No doubt you think I'm cruel, but then
Who invented the battery hen?'

I'm Going to be an Environmentalist When I Learn What to Do with the Greenfly

There's a gorilla in the wardrobe,
It must be from the zoo.
It's that or a fur-coat
Mum's hidden from view.
She's become a green
 Environmental Mum,
  Now she'll not be seen dead
   With that gorilla on!

Down in the garden,
Hidden in the shed,
Dad's gone and stashed away
A tatty fox's head.
 He's become a green
  Preservational Dad.
   All those baby foxes
    Must be feeling glad!

I hear that spraying greenfly
Is an environmental issue,
So I've been round the garden
Wrapping them in tissue.
I'd be as green as anyone
If I knew what to do.
Should I squeeze the greenfly gently
Or flush them down the loo?

The Mouse's Invitation Cards

'Come at seven,' 'Come at nine,'
'Come whenever you want.'
On the shelf the printed cards
Seem kind in their intent.

But the mouse will always stay at home,
He will never venture out,
No matter how the cards insist
Friends are all about.

One's from a cat, one's from an owl,
And both are intent
To draw him from his nest and then
Have him where they want.

Ten Angels Alone on Trapezes

I saw ten angels alone on trapezes,
Nine monkeys dancing in fire,
I saw eight snowflakes falling in lakes
And seven fish caught on a wire.

I saw six pirates with sacks full of treasure,
Five tigers sharing a crust,
Four budgerigars playing guitars
And three blackthorns covered in dust.

I saw two shadows without any owners,
One faded and then was gone,
Its friend searched for it in the darkness,
And then, of course, there were none.

The Pet Wig

Our teacher has a pet wig,
Nobody knows its name,
It crouches on his head all day
And looks extremely tame.

It's very calm and patient.
When dogs are on the prowl
It pretends it cannot hear the way
They clear their throats and growl.

It comes from a far-off land
(Or so we like to think),
A strange, endangered species
That's just about extinct.

After school he takes it off
And offers it some milk.
He strokes it extra gently
(Its fur is smooth as silk).

And in his lonely room at night
When he decides to retire,
He lays the wig quite carefully
On a blanket near the fire

Where after a long day clinging,
It rests content and purring.

The Race to Get to Sleep

They're on their marks, they're set,
They're off!

Matthew's kicking off his shoes!
Penny's struggling out of her jumper!
He's ripping off his trousers!
She's got one sock off! Now the other's off!
But Matthew's still winning! No, he's not!
It's Penny! Penny's in the lead!
She's down to her knickers!
She's racing out of the room!
She's racing upstairs!
Matthew's right behind her!
There's a fight on the landing!
There's a scramble at the bathroom door!
It's Penny! It's Matthew! It's…
Splash! They're both in the bath!
But there's a hitch!
Matthew's got soap in his eye!
Penny's got soap up her nose!
They're stalling! But no, they're both fine!
They're both out the bath! They're neck and neck!
It's Matthew! It's Penny! It's Matthew!

Now it's Penny again! She's ahead!
She's first on with her pyjamas!
Now Matthew's catching up! There's nothing in it!
They're climbing into their beds!
Matthew's in the lead with one eye closed!
Now it's Penny again! She's got both closed!
So's Matthew! He's catching up!
It's impossible to tell who's winning!
They're both absolutely quiet!
There's not a murmur from either of them.
It's Matthew! It's Penny! It's…
It's a draw! A draw!
But no! Wait a moment! It's not a draw!
Matthew's opened an eye!
He's asking if Penny's asleep yet!
He's disqualified!
So's Penny! She's doing the same!
She's asking if Matthew's asleep yet!
It's impossible! It's daft!
It's the hardest race in the world!

Gran Says

Gran says her friend Pat
Has a bee in her bonnet.
So I smeared honey on it.

Gran says her friend Mary
Is thick as two short planks.
She isn't. She's fat as two ten-ton tanks.

Gran says her friend Alice
Is always carrying a grudge.
I looked in her shopping-bag –
There wasn't one measly little Grudge in it.
I said, 'Don't budge, you've lost your Grudge!
Make sure Mary doesn't sit on it!
Catch it with Pat's sticky bonnet!'
Everyone thought I was mad.

Gran says her friend Clare
Leads a dog's life.
If so, why did she spit out
The winnowmeat sandwich I made her?

Gran says her friend Stan
Has a chip on his shoulder.
It's not true. When I saw him, I said,
'Has someone eaten your chip, Stan?'
He sort of frowned at Gran.

Gran says her friend Arthur
Thinks he's Lord Muck.
So that's what I called him
(And I bowed).
I don't know why Gran and
      him rowed.

Gran says her friend Joan
Needs her head examined.
Last time I saw her, I said,
'Sorry to hear about the nits.'

Now, whenever I visit Gran,
If her friends are there
She has fits.

Growing Groany

Grown-ups are groan-ups, there's no doubt about it,
You can tell by the way they groan on about it.

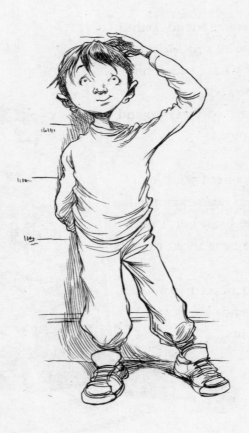

It's Poisoning Down

Gran keeps telling stories
Of how she used to go
Walking in the pouring rain
And playing in the snow.

She says that lakes and rivers
Were once all clean and pure,
I don't believe a word she says,
I've heard it all before.

Poor Gran can be quite dotty –
You want to see Mum frown
When Gran tries to get outside
Even though it's poisoning down.

We've had to fit 'Granny Locks'
To keep poor Granny in.
She really doesn't understand
How rain eats away the skin.

The Milk-shake Café

I went into the milk-shake café
And saw the milk-shake cows,
They stood behind the counter
In different-flavoured rows.

The banana-flavoured milk-shake cow
Ate bananas by the bunch,
The raspberry-flavoured milk-shake cow
Had raspberries for lunch.

The lemon-flavoured milk-shake cow
Sulked and spat out pips,
The orange-flavoured milk-shake cow
Had orange-coloured lips.

To get the milk-shakes frothy
There was s strange machine
That shook the mooing cows
And turned their milk to cream.

There were so many different flavours
We were spoilt for choice,
Until one day the owner said
In a trembly sort of voice,

'Quick! Clear out the café.
I've just been told today,
The place is being raided
By the RSPCA.'

Mary Had a Bit of Lamb

Mary had a little lamb,
Its fleece was white as snow,
And everywhere that Mary went
The lamb was sure to go.

She went into the butcher's,
Came out with some lamb chops.
I would never follow Mary
Into any kind of shops!

Flies in Disguise

On a currant bun
wise flies
hide in disguise.

Playing Football with the Dog

Arthur Sneer played football with his dog.
How cruel can you get?

Dirty Laugh

The reason I've never seen a
Clean hyena
Is because instead of bath-night
They have a laugh-night.

Schoolitis

You haven't got a cough,
You haven't got mumps,
You haven't got a chill
Or any funny lumps.
You haven't got a tummy-ache,
You haven't got a fever,
You haven't got a runny nose
Or chicken-pox either.
You don't look a ruin,
You don't look a wreck.
You haven't got toothache
Or a pain in the neck.
You're as fit as a fiddle,
You're as sound as a bell,
In fact I've never ever
Seen you looking so well!
You don't fool me,
I'm no fool.
Now up out of bed
AND OFF TO SCHOOL!

How the New Teacher Got Her Nickname

When the new teacher said,
'I'm going to be frank with you,'
I burst out laughing.
'What are you laughing about?' she asked.
'It's hard to explain, Frank,' I said.
From that moment on Miss Jones became Frank.
For that she has me to thank.

'I Want a Word With You Lot...'

'I want a word with you lot,'
Declared the new Head.
'We hope the word's tasty,'
The cheeky class said.
'We hope it's not *sprout*,
Or *cabbage* or *fish*,
Or anything healthy poured into a dish.
A good word would be *sausage*,
or *chocolate*, or *pie*,
And *cake* is a word
For which we'd all die.'

'It's none of those words,
But I'll give you a clue –
It slips from your heads
And it's long overdue.
The word that I want
Is not one word, but two
That when stuck together
Make you feel blue.
You all know it well,
You loathe it, you shirk
From facing up to
That word
        HOMEWORK!'

Grumbly Moon

'Turn that music down!'
shouted the grumbly moon to
the rock 'n' roll stars.

Runny Egg

For breakfast I had a runny egg.
I chased it round the table.
It wobbled and it screeched at me,
'Catch me if you're able!'

So I nailed it to the table.

The Cook's Tragedy
A Short Play for Ham Actors

A: I once knew a cook who moved among the cream
   of society.

B: A good egg?

A: Unfortunately he thought he could have his cake
   and eat it.

B: You mean he wanted everything on a plate?

A: Exactly. He thought life was going to be as easy
   as pie.

B: Obviously he never used his loaf.

A: One day, when the chips were down, he turned sour.

B: I suppose he became a fast liver?

A: He didn't give a sausage for anyone.

B: No doubt he ended up in the soup?

A: Of course. He realised his goose was cooked when
   he heard the police had a bone to pick with him.

B: You mean he was acting fishy and they grilled him?

A: He told them a half-baked story and they gave him
   a real roasting.

B: Such lives are food
   for thought.

Sleepy-time Crime

I looked in the mirror,
Had a bit of a scare,
For when I looked closer
I wasn't there.

I turned round to find if
I was behind me,
But when I turned round
I couldn't find me.

'I've vanished!' I thought,
'I'm gone for ever!
I shouldn't have been
Such a big bother!

No one will find me
Or miss me or care.
The mirror is empty.
I am not there!'

I pondered and wondered
And then I remembered
The thing I had done
While everyone slumbered:

I'd sneaked from my room
Dressed up as a Viking
To see if my outfit
Was quite to my liking.

I'd adjusted the mirror
On its nail on the wall,
Never expecting
The daft thing to fall.

CRASH! went the mirror,
But no one had woken!
So I hid all the pieces
Of the mirror I'd broken.

Then I sneaked back to bed
To worry and sleep,
And then up again
For a guilt-ridden peep.

I wished I'd only dreamt
That I had broken
The mirror I'd broken
When no one had woken,

But my crime stared me
Right not in the face;
No doubt in the morning
I'll be in disgrace.

Hide-away Sam

Hide-away Sam sat in the darkness,
Pale as the day he was born,
A miser who stored up his blessings
Yet looked on blessings with scorn.

He peeked through a chink in the doorway,
A crack on which the sun shone.
All the things he had craved danced past him,
He blinked, and they were gone.

A ladder was stretched up to Heaven,
Its rungs were covered in dew,
At its foot was a bucket of diamonds
(From the sky God had stolen a few)

And beyond the ladder was an orchard
Where bees dunked in pollen flew
Between the falling blossom
And the core of a fruit that was new.

'Time to come out and enjoy life!'
A voice boomed down from above.
'Time to swap ten aeons of darkness
For one bright second of love.'

But Hide-away Sam shrank inwards.
He refused to open the door.
The Angel of Mercy lost patience,
Shrugged, and said no more.

Hushabye Lullaby

Listen. Hush.
Don't be hasty.
Something's eating
Something tasty.

In the cupboard
As lights go off
Can't you hear
Moths chomping cloth?

Listen. Hush.
Other sounds
Are moonlight falling
On the ground,

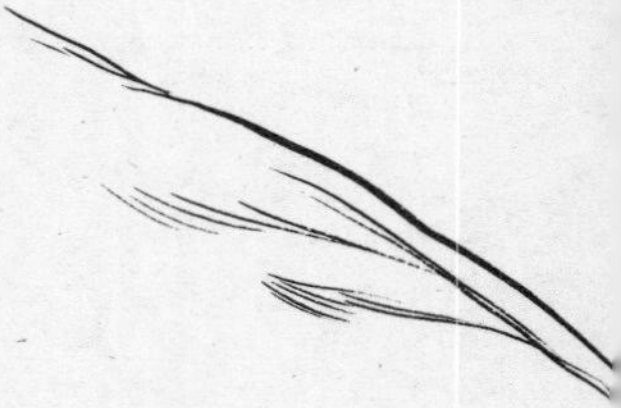

And shadows bumping
Into trees,
And the snoring,
Dreaming bees.

Listen. Hush.
Isn't that
The soft pad
Of the cat?

There are sounds
I am not sure
I have ever
Heard before.

I try so hard
To hear all things
Behind the silence
That sleep brings.

Rabbit's Spring

Snow
goes,

Ice
thaws,

Warm
paws!

Growing Pains

Growing
      bored
Growing
      sad
Growing
      mad
Growing
      batty
Growing
      scatty
Looking
      tatty
Feeling
      ratty
Looking
      frumpy
Growing
      jumpy
Feeling
      grumpy
Growing
      spotty
Growing
      Pains

Rebellion on the Catwalk

The snake-skin hissed, 'I hate this show!'
The leopard-skin said it did too.
The fox-fur said, 'I concur.
I'm leaving, how about you?'

The clothes the crowd had been wearing
Cried out, 'Enough is enough!
We never wore human skin –
We could do without that stuff.'

The clothes struggled free of their captors,
There was a sudden uproar
As with revitalised grins the fur-coats and the skins
Rushed out of the exit door.

The audience were astonished.
They were left half-naked and cold –
The young, the fat, the flabby,
The tall, the skinny, the old.

'My leather trousers are gone!
I feel silly and chilly!
I've only my hat left
To cover my willy!'
'Where's my leopard-skin dress?
My bra looks a mess!
Please turn away,
My knickers are grey!'

There was quite a commotion,
Everyone felt such a fool,
Except a young usherette in a nice
   cotton dress
Who said, 'I couldn't care less –
Killing for fashion is cruel.'

51

The Church Rat

A rat lived in my brother's shoe,
It was a lonely creature.
I took it to a church one day
And gave it to a preacher.

It ate the bread, it drank the wine,
It nibbled on a cassock,
It grew a little tipsy
And caused a lot of havoc.

'Dear rat, calm down! Control yourself.
You are in the presence of a preacher.'
'I know,' it said. 'In another life
I was the preacher's teacher.'

'I do believe you're right,' I said.
'There's a similarity in the way
You hold your paws and he his hands
When you both bend down to pray.'

The Secret Prayer

There's a prayer I never tell my mum and dad.
Even when I hate them, I say it just the same.
'Dear God,
Don't ever let them die, or if you do
Make sure I go too.
Or better still, wait until I'm gone
Then let them follow on –
Because without them Heaven would
Not be half as good.'

Michael Monday

Born on Monday, Tuesday see
Me going to the nursery.
Wednesday finds me at the gate
Of the school I love to hate.
Thursday finds me blushing pink.
(I'm in love again, I think.)
Friday finds upon my knee
A child that belongs to me.
By Saturday I'm wrinkling up,
On Sunday I run out of puff.
Then Monday comes around again
And I am free of Sunday's pain.
Now I am another thing
And sit up in a tree and sing,
And see the world a different way
To how I saw it yesterday.

Why Toads Look Much More Serious Than Frogs

Between croaks
frogs on logs
crack jokes.
It tantalises
flies and loads
of toads.
In their abodes
between croaks
these sombre blokes
analyse the jokes.

Blind Hope

A frog crawled out of the marshland,
Sat on a mound of earth,
To the creatures gathered round him
He boasted of his worth.

'I'm a fantastic doctor,
There's nothing I can't heal,
If you are ever sick
To me you can appeal.'

The animals stared amazed
At his blotched, spotty skin,
At his huge and bulging eyes
And legs so long and thin.

'Boastful fool, go crawl back home –
You ought to see your face!
You're a small and slimy frog
That ought to know its place!'

56

His puffed-up pride was injured,
He thought them most ill-bred,
He turned to face them slyly
And this stark truth he said:

'No doubt there will come a day
When no doctor is near –
Then you'll forget I'm a frog –
Blind hope will drive you here.'

What do you Want with your Chips?

Do you want cat stew with mint sauce,
    putrid plums and cream,
Or custard-coated crushed canaries
    held in high esteem?

We can serve hedgehog and fried figs
    or poodle-pup pie,
Or a rack of roasted rats' tails
    straight from Paraguay.

…Er. I think I'll just have the
    chips, please.

Bits and Pieces

When Uncle Fredrick passed away
It really broke our hearts,
He loved going to the hospital
To be fitted with spare parts.

After the wake we made a list
Then sat about and mused
Over all the bits and pieces
That might still be used.

We set out to find them.
It caused no great alarm
To find in the cupboard
His artificial arm.

'Three cheers for Uncle Fredrick!'
Was the merry mourners' shout.
'We've found a bit of Fredrick.
Now there's less to grieve about.'

We searched inside the cupboard
To dispel our lingering grief,
On the bottom shelf we found
A set of stained false teeth.

This cheered us up no end
And with less reason now to weep,
We tiptoed back into the room
Where Fredrick used to sleep.

On the bedside table
It came as no surprise
To find inside a glass jar
A spare set of his glass eyes.

Then from downstairs we heard
Another 'Hip hurray!
It's not the cat Gran's trodden on,
It's Fredrick's old toupee!'

But our excitement was diminished
And our eyes began to smart,
When we found the missing valve
From Uncle Fredrick's heart.

Still, we piled what we had gathered
In the centre of the room.
There were enough bits and pieces
To disperse the gloom.

So hip hip again for Fredrick,
If we go on like this
There will be nothing much of Fredrick
To either mourn or miss.

Aphasia *

I'm seven, and I'm dead bright,
But words give me a fright.
Words are bullies.
Sneaky things. They gabble and lie.
Sometimes trying to understand them
Makes me cry. Words hurt.
Words are all over the place,
They get shoved in my face.
I don't know why but
Words make me cry.

I wish words were things
You could hug.
Or that they smelt nice.
I wish they came in bottles
Like fizzy drinks, or melted
Like ice-cream. But they don't,
Words are mean. They bully me,
Lock me away
From what I want to say.

I can't even ask for help
And I'm only seven
(And a bit).
Words spread nasty gossip.
They must. Otherwise why
Would people think I'm thick.

Words.
They make me sick
Inside.

* Aphasia is a condition that makes it difficult for people
to understand or learn speech. It causes great distress.

Some Rhymes are a Sight and Some are Really Sound

It's a pity the sound of *cough*
Won't rhyme with *rough*.
It's tough.
And it's a bother that *Dover and cover*
Don't suit one another
While *clover and Rover*
Rhyme over and over.
It's odd
How *pot* and *lot* both rhyme with *squat*
But *squat* will not
Rhyme with *cat* despite the *at*.
Fancy that!
And though there's no *y* in *high*
It still rhymes with *fly*
And so will *sky* unless an *i*
Replaces the *y*

Which makes it *ski*
Which rhymes with *me*, you see?
The last example I'll cite
Is how *site* and *sight*
Both rhyme with *might*,
Though on the page *might*
Might look a sight
If rhymed with *cite*
So I'll put out the light.
Good night!

Winter Variations

GRASSHOPPERS

Grasshoppers bending blades of grass
Tomorrow will be coated in snow,

However much you want them to stay
The wind will snatch their songs away.

LEAVES

I heard the trees whispering, each tongue was a leaf,
And what they were whispering was, 'Stop, thief!'

Behind them Jack Frost was hurrying away.
In his hands each leaf had begun to decay.

BEES

Flightless bees, numbed by cold,
Leave winding trails in the sparkling frost,
Winter's a maze in which they're lost.

GOLDFISH

Beneath a sheet of milky ice,
Transformed by a wintry wand,

I saw phantom goldfish floating
Like sunken treasure in the pond.

Spider Apples

Someone told me recently
That I should never go
Into the glittering orchard
Now thick with frozen snow,

For there I'd meet a spider
Who would offer me
Frost-scented, ice-rimmed apples
Plucked from a burning tree,

And if I were to taste one
Then I would never be
Free of that glittering orchard
Where weird apples grow

And a cloven hoof-print
Is marked clearly in the snow.

My Sister, My Brothers, Christmas and Me

The reason our Cathy's crying
Isn't hard to understand,
She tugged at Santa's beard
And it came off in her hand.

When we dragged her out the grotto
We passed a butcher's shop.
She saw a row of headless turkeys
And then she cried non-stop.

It's Christmas! It's Christmas!
We're going to have some fun,
Mum is in a panic
And it's only just begun.

The goose is in the oven,
And so's the budgie too –
Its cage was opened by mistake
And that is where it flew.

A robin from the garden
Hopped in on to the mat.
It looked just like a Christmas card,
But now it's in the cat.

There'll be a thousand mince-pies
And lots of cream to lick,
There'll be so much of everything
I'm bound to get quite sick.

There'll be tangerines and walnuts,
Brandy pudding too,
Chocolate-coated angels
And toffees to chew.

Last year I got a boring book
From awful Aunty Jane.
This year I'm going to wrap it up
And send it back again.

For my horrid little brother
I don't know what to get.
I think I'll just wrap him up
And send him to the vet.

I'm fed up with his fingerprints
On all the pies and cake.
And the way he thinks my things
Were bought for him to break.

I wish Santa would come early
And stuff him in his sack –
He could take him to the North Pole
And never bring him back.

He could leave him in an igloo,
I'm sure no one would care.
He'd make a rather tasty snack
For a [hungry] polar bear.

My older brother scoffs at me.
He's made a nasty trap.
He says if Santa does exist
We're bound to hear it snap.

I've just written off to warn him,
And have explained how to defuse
The electric cable on the roof
My brother says he'll use.

He'd demobilise the reindeers,
Fry Santa in his sleigh,
He'd do some really awful things
If he could have his way.

But Christmas is a time of love,
And so we've called a truce.
Now everyone will be happy...
Except for the goose.

Hippo-rhyme-opotamus

'I'm sick to death,' the hippo said,
'I tell you, there are times
I'd like to crush those awful poets
And all their silly rhymes.
It really is undignified
The way they rhyme my name.
I wish I was magnanimous
But I feel venomous
When my name's made synonymous
With people like Hieronymous.
It's absolutely scurrilous
How their half-baked rhymes mock at us
Harmless hippopotamus.

Small Wonders

Brand-new elephant roamed through the jungles.
Brand-new whales splashed down through the oceans.
God had slapped them together,
Happy as a kid making mud pies.

He wiped His hands clean.
'Now for the hard part,' He thought.
He took his workbench into the garden.
Delicately He placed in
    the bee's sting.
The moth's antenna.
Into the salmon He placed
The memory of an ocean,
His hand not trembling
    in the slightest.

The Soldier's Shoe
After a poem by Morgenstern

Along the road one cold war-torn dawn
Wandered a shoe with an old shoe-horn.

The shoe was empty but with a cough
It begged and pleaded, 'Please pull me off.'

The shoe-horn said, 'Hang on a minute,
You're just a shoe with nothing in it.

I do not want to be cruel, or scoff,
But there's nothing left to pull you off.

The reason you look bloody and red
Is that your foot's been blown up, it's dead.'

The shoe said, 'Fancy that, well I'll be blowed!'
And they continued on up the road.

Don't Forget to Wash Behind your Hearing-aid!

It's hard getting your own back on groan-ups.
When I was young
I always thought
one of the best things about
being grown up would be
getting my own back on those who
had been nasty to me.
But groan-ups cheat.
While you are busy growing up
they think: 'Hu, hu, there's that boy
I was nasty to, and he's nearly
old enough to get his own back!'
They feel they're under attack
and start to shrink. I think
they do it on purpose. They get
all frail and wizeny-looking
and you just can't go around
getting your own back on little old ladies
and wrinkly little men
who were nasty when
you were eight or nine or ten.

You can't twist their ears
or shake them by the shoulder
and shout, 'Take your teeth out!
And brush them immediately!'
or
'Don't forget to wash behind your hearing-aid!'
The trouble is you don't even want to.
Groan-ups always win.
It's one of the hard, hard facts of life.

The Devil of a Cook

I've never cooked a crocodile,
I'm not partial to boiled bear,
I've never fried a fox-cub
(Think of all that fur).

I've never whisked a weasel
Or mashed a mongoose,
I've never poached a pelican
In the bladder of a moose.

I've never sautéed snakes
Or guzzled grilled gazelle,
I've never tried to toast
A tortoise in its shell.

Liquidizing lizards
And microwaving mice
Might be stylish cooking
But they don't taste very nice.

Grating baby glow-worms
Or mincing death's-head moths
Does nothing for my taste-buds.
(I can't stand insect broths.)

78

Though I've baked a badger
And casseroled a chimp
Sitting down and eating them
Would make my bowels go limp.

I'm the devil of a cook,
The animals know me well.
I fry their souls for breakfast
In my kitchen down in hell.

Take-away Nightmare

In the local lip-smackin' Deep-fried Human Shop
I asked for something tasty, said, 'How about a chop?'

The chicken that was serving dished up food non-stop.
'Do you want one on its own?' it asked, 'or with peas
    on top?'

'How about the taste?' I asked. 'I'm not exactly sure
I fancy eating humans. I've not tried one before.'

'They taste like your mother, they taste like your dad,
They're as tender as your sister, in fact they're not
    that bad.'

I dithered and dawdled, not sure what to eat.
The animal behind me suggested human feet.

'They have a decent flavour, especially the toes.
They're my favourite bit of humans – I'm having two
    of those.'

In the local lip-smackin' Deep-fried Human Shop
I saw a plate of baby's brains with hot sauce on top.

Of course it was a nightmare, I'd not gone insane,
But still I won't be eating take-aways again.

Little Miss Look-at-me

I went for a picnic,
I went down to the beach,
I was going to have a lazy day
Until I heard that screech:
                    'Look-at-me!'

It was Little Miss Look-at-me,
She was yelling all the time,
'Look-at-me! Look-at-me!'
As if it were a crime
To look at something else instead
Of looking all the time
At that little prima donna
Who thought she was sublime.

She was splashing in the water,
Moving out of reach,
Ignoring all the children
Scrambling for the beach
                    Because...

Quick! Get out of the water!
'Look-at-me! Look-at-me!'
Will you shut up and listen? There's a
'Look-at-me! Look-at-me!'
Huge shark coming and it's
'Look-at-me! Look-at-me!'
Getting closer and
'Look-at-me! Look-at-me!'
closer and
'Look-at-me! Look-at-me!'
ITS TEETH ARE SHARP AND WHITE AND

Whoops!

Little Miss Look-at-me
In the belly of a shark,
Haven't heard a word from her
And it's getting rather dark,

So think I'll go back home
And take a nap in bed,
Now there's no more
    Miss Look-at-me
Jangling in my head.

You Can't Be That

I told them:
When I grow up
I'm not going to be a scientist
Or someone who reads the news on TV.
No, a million birds will fly through me.
I'm going to be a tree!

They said,
You can't be that. No, you can't be that.

I told them:
When I grow up
I'm not going to be an airline pilot,
A dancer, a lawyer or an MC.
No, huge whales will swim in me.
I'm going to be an ocean!

They said,
You can't be that. No, you can't be that.

I told them:
I'm not going to be a DJ,
A computer programmer, a musician or a beautician.
No, streams will flow through me, I'll be the home of
    eagles:
I'll be full of nooks, crannies, valleys and fountains.
I'm going to be a range of mountains!

They said,
You can't be that. No, you can't be that.

I asked them:
Just what do you think I am?
Just a child, they said,
And children always become
At least one of the things
We want them to be.

They do not understand me.
I'll be a stable if I want, smelling of fresh hay,
I'll be a lost glade in which unicorns still play.
They do not realise I can fulfil any ambition.
They do not realise among them
Walks a magician.

Short-sighted Sergeant Urgent
or, Detergent's No Deterrent

Sergeant Urgent swiftly shopping
Through the supermarket rushing,
Among the soap suds and the polish
Misread 'detergent' as 'deterrent'.

He shouted out to the shoppers,
'This'll put the cop back into coppers!
It'll rub the rob right out of robbers
And a million other thieves and bothers!'

Excitedly, Sergeant Urgent
Bought ten tons of the detergent.
Poor short-sighted Sergeant Urgent,
He used it all but sad to say
The crooks he caught got clean
away.

The Utter Butter Nutter

Herbert Niggins was a nutter,
On the staircase he spread butter.
We knew he was a real twit
When he went and slipped on it.

Llama Calmer

Never alarm a harmless llama
But try to calm an alarmed llama
Because a calm llama will never harm a
Hair on the head of a llama calmer.

The Daft Owl

Not all owls go
'Tu-whit, tu-whoo'
(It's not something
All owls do).
I knew one whoo
Was tu-whit

less

    tu-

        whoo.

The Rival Arrives

Tom, take the baby out the fridge
And put the milk back in.
We know you are not used to him
And think he makes a din,
But I'm afraid he's here to stay
And he is rather cute,
So you'll have to stop insisting
He goes in the car-boot.
And please stop telling all your friends
We bought him in a sale,
Or that he's a free sample
We received in the mail.
He was not found in a trolley
At the local Mothercare,
And a family did not give him us
Because they'd one to spare.

You should look on the bright side, Tom.
In just a year or two
You will have someone
    else to blame
For the wicked things you do.

The World's Most Disgusting Medicine or, Never Kick the Doctor in the Shin

Dad's after-shave and rattlesnake's spit,
A monkey's tongue (but only a bit),
Super-glue and Bostik, kangaroo vomit,
Maggoty old mole-fur with dead fleas on it.
Snails crushed in pepper-grinders, fungus from a rat,
A milky-white eye from a dead tabby cat,
Slime from the bottom of an old dustbin,
Two little cockroaches crushed up thin,
Juice from a cabbage boiled for a year,
Squishy smelly wax from an elephant's ear.
These are the ingredients the doctor put in
The medicine he gave me when I kicked him in the shin.

Sally Slipshod

Miss Sally Slipshod lost her memory
One bright sparkling autumn day,
She tried to pick up a burning sunbeam,
Was amazed it got away.

Saw a birch tree; thought it a fountain
Tumbling through the space between
The garden wall and rhododendron
Where the birch tree had once been.

She mistook a child for an angel,
Mistook a rose for its wounds:
The busy world's bald din and clatter
Was transformed to tinkling sounds.

The dawn transformed earth's clods to diamonds,
Wind orchestrated the bars
Of the spiky branches in which clung
The frosty blossoms of stars.

These were the things her memory clung to,
The rest she let fall away.
She saw God's kind face in each spider's;
She knelt among them to pray.

When darkness fell she did not see it;
Saw only light flowing there.
'Your mind has gone wrong,' people warned her.
Sally Slipshod did not care.

How could dull people comprehend her?
Ears so sharp they could unveil
The sound of water in a mountain
And from two miles the nightingale.

Miss Sally Slipshod lost the memory
Of all things dark, drab and dull,
And of the prison others made for
All she considered wonderful.

Swap Shop

Coming home from school one day
I saw to my surprise
A sign saying Swap Shop
Right there before my eyes.

Could I swap my sister Kate?
Could I swap my brother Hugh?
We'd been squabbling for ages.
I fancied something new.

Excitedly I wrapped Kate up
And took her to the shop.
"How about my sister here –
What'll you give me if I swap?"

"We'll give you a ton of gold," they said,
"Two leopards and a talking cat.
We'll give you a bunch of fabulous jewels
For a sister such as that."

"If she's worth so much I'll take her back,
She must be the very best.
I'll bring along my brother instead -
He's a little pest."

"For him - a can of worms," they said,
"Two mouse-skins and a bat.
We'll give you a clout on the ear," they said,
"If you bring a brat like that."

Sandwiches

It's not the sea muttering
Or the crabs carousing,
Or salty shrimps singing
Or flying fish sighing
For all their friends frying –
                    No!
It's sandwiches dancing
And prancing and cackling!
Sandwiches picnicking,
O it's quite sickening
The spells that they're whispering!
'Eat us!' they're muttering
And all the while buttering
Each other and muttering
Strange spells into sea-shells
And what is much worse is
They're cursing the nurses
Who came to the beaches
With children and teachers
And various creatures
Who ate juicy peaches
But left the sandwiches
Curled up at the edges

Alone on the beaches
In sea-storms and blizzards
Nibbled by wizards
Disguised as sand-lizards.
Listen to them calling!
They sound quite appalling:
'O we'll get our T back
Until then the hitch is
We're harmless
        sandwiches
Instead of SAND
        WITCHES!'

Birds

You might know about the yaffle,
The culver and the widgeon –
All a bit more exciting than
That boring bird, the pigeon.

How about the cassowary?
The apteryx? The moa?
Those flightless birds next to whom
Most others run much slower.

There is nothing beats the eagle,
Or the falcon or the kite,
When it comes to acrobatics
They excel themselves in flight.

Some other birds mistrust the sky
And think that water's grander.
I am thinking now of the swan,
The ouzel and goosander.

It is true the parrot's boastful
And speaks a lot of rot
And insists on being filthy
When his owners wish he'd not.

He's really not my favourite bird.
I suppose that at a push
My favourite bird would be the wren
If it sang more like the thrush.

Let's not say much about the dodo,
The poor thing is obsolete.
One reason is because it was
Baked by pirates as a treat.

Today the saddest birds of all
Must be the hen and turkey.
Their lives are brief, their futures
Look extremely murky.

In recent times the safest bird
Has become the cooing dove,
For who on this earth will admit
To a taste for killing Love?

Chilly Hot

Mum said, 'Careful!
Rice is chilly.'
I said, 'No, it's not.
Don't be silly.'
When my mouth caught fire
Mum laughed a lot –
The rice wasn't chilly
But the chilli was hot.

Magic Breath

In the park one winter I was caught out in a storm,
I blew upon my hands – just to make them warm.

Coming home exhausted from a gruelling day at school,
I blew upon my soup – just to make it cool.

I must be a magician! Why was I never told
That with a single breath I can
Blow both hot and cold?

There's an Old Town

There's an old town where nobody goes,
Where nobody lives, where there's never a noise.
We pass through it in motors, above it in planes,
We clatter right past it in the safety of trains.
There's no milkman, no postman, no policeman either,
No schoolyard, or playground, not even a teacher.
Few people go there and none come away,
There's no one to play with at the end of the day.
In it are angels and demons and stones
That lean close together
   and whisper of bones.

Speared Peer
An Elocution lesson

Last year
On a pier
near Tangier
for reasons unclear
I fear
an austere racketeer
from Agadir
stabbed a peer
in the rear
with a spear.

My Friend Wazinme

'I don't know how he did it,
But my friend Wazinme
Snapped the two main branches off
Dad's brand-new cherry tree.'

'Are you sure it was not you
Who broke the cherry tree?'
'Of course,' I said, 'it was my friend,
You know it Wazinme!'

Thawing Frozen Frogs

Last autumn Jimmy, for a wheeze,
Tried out our mum's new deep-freeze.
He suddenly made up his mind
To freeze all the frogs he could find.
He packed and stored them all away,
Then brought them out again today.
But he lost interest and grew bored
The very moment that they thawed.
For they did not blink or croak or leap
And from their mouths there seemed to seep
Some disgusting slimy matter
That leaked into Mum's cooking batter.
She found the frogs and, feeling sick,
Rushed to the bathroom rather quick.
You should have heard the way
        Dad roared,
'Scrape those frogs from the
        draining-board!'
After Dad's investigation
Other crimes came
        to attention
And in between protests and wails
Jimmy dug out the worms and snails.

The River's Story

I remember when life was good.
I shilly-shallied across meadows,
Tumbled down mountains,
I laughed and gurgled through woods,
Stretched and yawned in a myriad of floods.
Insects, weightless as sunbeams,
Settled upon my skin to drink.
I wore lily-pads like medals.
Fish, lazy and battle-scarred,
Gossiped beneath them.
The damselflies
    were my
    ballerinas,
The pike my
    ambassadors.
Kingfishers, disguised
    as rainbows,
Were my secret agents.

It was a sweet time, a gone-time,
A time before factories grew,
Brick by greedy brick,
And left me cowering in monstrous shadows.
Like drunken giants
They vomited their poisons into me.
Tonight a scattering of vagrant bluebells,
Dwarfed by those same poisons,
Toll my ending.
Children, come and find me if you wish,
I am your inheritance.
Behind the derelict housing-estates
You will discover my remnants.
Clogged with garbage and junk
To an open sewer I've shrunk.
I, who have flowed through history,
Who have seen hamlets become villages,
Villages become towns, towns become cities,
Am reduced to a trickle of filth
Beneath the still, burning stars.

Dad Remembers his Schooldays

When the teacher who used
To yell at us and cane us left
We held a secret collection.
Billy Owen passed around
A brown paper bag.
We filled it, hardly able
To keep straight faces.
At the very last second of
The very last minute of
The very last hour of
The spring term,
We sneaked our bags of gifts
Into his desk and flowed
Out of the school-gates and into summer.
The bag contained a crushed earwig,
A pen-nib, fingernail cuttings,
A rude drawing, a dead wasp,
And, weird as it may sound,
A moth's wing found
In the playground.
Screwed up inside the bag
was a note saying,
'Good riddance to that pain,
Mr McCane.'

The next term he was gone.
The paper bag was gone.
Life went on.
It was only years later that,
Quite suddenly, I remembered him –
Not as the giant, fearsome McCane,
But as a little man,
Mean and thin.
And I wondered what became of him,
And how he must have felt
When he found our gifts,
The tokens of esteem
In which we held him.
I felt sorry for him.
You see, by then I had forgotten
The sting of his cane.

Nancy Noah

Three by three they came in,
All the clatter, all the din!
Two for the world when it was dry,
One to boil or bake or fry,
Mrs Noah had a cooking-pot
And she served up dinner
    piping-hot.

Three by three they came in,
Some were fat and some were thin.
The couples were easy but it was harder
Getting the rest into the larder.

'Hurry along! Walk! Don't fly!'
Said this evening's pigeon-pie.
'You hop first.' 'No, after you,'
Said tomorrow's rabbit-stew.

Three by three they came in,
All the clatter, all the din!
Two for the world when it was dry,
One to boil or bake or fry.
Mrs Noah had a cooking-pot
And she served up dinner piping-hot.

The Pint-sized Ark

William stood in the encroaching dark
Banging nails into a pint-sized Ark.
People gathered round him and they mocked
Each single nail mad William knocked
Into the Ark, the pint-sized Ark,
Standing in the encroaching dark
Between the tower-blocks and park.

William, banging, what's it for?
Don't you know it's been done before?

A policeman came, and he made a note:
'It's hardly the size of a rowing-boat.
The Ark's so small he will hardly get
Himself in along with the family pet.'

True, thought William, but my soul will fit,
And that's all I need get into it.

BANG BANG drip BANG BANG drip
BANG drip BANG BANG drip BANG drip

His face was vacant, in his eye was a spark,
And his hammer beat in time to the encroaching dark.

To Join Our Club

To join our club you've got to
Climb a mountain, swim a sea,
Be back home in time for tea.

Easy

That's just the first thing.
To join our club you've got to
Pull a bulldog by the tail,
Catch and eat a garden snail.

OK

That's just the second thing.
To join our club you must
Thrill a gorilla, whack a yak,
Paint your bedroom entirely black.

No problem

That's just the third thing.
To join our club you must
Nail a pixie to a rose,
Twist its ear and pick its nose.

I'll do it right away

That's just the fourth thing.
To join our club you must
a)   Be kind to your sister.
b)   Wash up after supper.
c)   Do your homework.
d)   Not watch so much TV.

That's not the club for me.

Dear Mum,

while you were out a cup went and broke itself,
a crack appeared in that blue vase
your great-grandad
brought back from Mr Ming in China.
Somehow, without me even turning on the tap,
the sink mysteriously overflowed
And a strange jam-stain the size of a boy's hand
appeared on the kitchen wall.
I don't think we will ever discover
exactly how the cat
managed to turn on the washing-machine
(especially from the inside),
or how our pet rabbit went and mistook
the waste disposal unit for a burrow.
Also, Mum, I know the canary looks grubby,
but it took me ages
getting it out of the vacuum-cleaner.

I was being good
(honest)
but I think the house is haunted so,
knowing you're going to have a fit,
I've gone over to Gran's to lie low for a bit.

Unstable Mabel

Mabel's unstable, be careful, beware
Of that look in her eyes that says,
  'I don't care.
I'll do what I want, however unfair.'
Mabel's unstable, and isn't all there.
Mabel's unstable, and able I'm sure
To nail up an angel on to the back door.
Somebody must take her far, far away.
That's what we long for, and pray for each day.
No one remembers from where Mabel came.
Found on the doorstep and brought in from the rain
She sat in a corner, glowered and moaned,
'I was raised by a man whose head was horned.'
Mabel's unstable and if you want proof
Look down at her foot. You'll find only a hoof.
Her eyes are ablaze, like cinders, like fire,
And her dark hair is tangled like razor-sharp wire.

Sad Kisses

Don't want to kiss anyone ever.
I've seen Mum and Dad do it.
Before you do it
You shout at one another,
Then you hit one another,
Then you cry,
Then you kiss and make up.
Kissing must hurt.
It's horrible.

First Love

Sarah's my girlfriend,
Without her I feel
Like a ball with no bounce,
A shoe with no heel,
An up with no down,
A snow with no flake,
A fish trying to swim
In a waterless lake.
Sarah's my girlfriend,
Without her I fear
I feel that I'm nowhere,
Especially not here.

Mr and Mrs No

Mr and Mrs No had nowhere to live,
They had nothing to do and nothing to give;
They lived in no house in no pleasant street,
And had nowhere to go and no one to meet.
They did nothing wrong and they did nothing right,
Nobody saw them or knew them by sight,
When dawn came around they were nowhere about;
If they existed, nobody found out.

The Irreplaceable Mum

If you were a crack in a mirror,
If you were a flea on a cat,
If you were a slug in a jug,
I'd still love you, I wouldn't mind that.

If you were a smudge on a picture
Or an opera singer struck dumb,
If you were a pain in the
    neck then
You'd still be my very
    best chum.

If you were a fly in
    a pizza,
If you were a
    difficult sum,
Even if you were
    humpy and
    grumpy
You'd still be
    irreplaceable,
    Mum.

Brian Patten was born in Liverpool and made his name
as one of the Liverpool Poets. His first anthology, with
Roger McGough and Adrian Henri, *The Mersey Sound*,
has been credited as the most significant anthology of
the 20th century in bringing poetry to a new audience.
His children's collections include *Gargling with Jelly* and
Juggling with Gerbils, and he is the editor of *The Puffin
Book of 20th Century Children's Verse* and *The Puffin Book of
Utterly Brilliant Poetry*. He has been honoured with
the Freedom of the City of Liverpool and is a
Fellow of the Royal Society of Literature, and of
Liverpool University and John Moore's University.
He lives in London and Devon.

Chris Riddell was born in Liverpool and is a highly
acclaimed writer and illustrator of children's books.
He has twice won the Kate Greenaway Award, and the
Smarties prize seven times. His books for Frances Lincoln
include *Out for the Count* with Katherine Cave and
Until I Met Dudley with Roger McGough.
He is also a cartoonist for The Observer.
He lives in Brighton.

MORE POETRY FROM
FRANCES LINCOLN CHILDREN'S BOOKS

978-1-84780-166-1 • PB • £5.99

An A-Z of animal poems with a difference!
Choose your favourite from Roger McGough's
witty and wicked menagerie.

"Classic Roger McGough" – *Guardian*

978-1-84780-321-4 • PB • £5.99

This brilliant collection is full of wit,
wordplay and wisdom from Roger McGough...

"A word juggler who never misses a catch"
Charles Causley

978-1-84780-169-2 • PB • £5.99

From spooky legends to dreamy poems, teasers
and rhymes, expect the unexpected. A poetry adventure
waiting to happen!

"A poet with a powerful feeling for story and language" –
Carousel

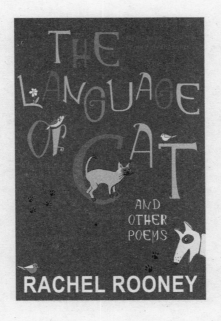

978-1-84780-167-8 • PB • £5.99

With wordplay and riddles, and poems that will make
you laugh, tell you stories and make you think, this is
a brilliant debut from an exciting new poet.

"A box of delights" – *Carol Ann Duffy*